YOUR KNOWLEDGE HAS VALUE

- We will publish your bachelor's and master's thesis, essays and papers

- Your own eBook and book - sold worldwide in all relevant shops

- Earn money with each sale

Upload your text at www.GRIN.com
and publish for free

Bibliographic information published by the German National Library:

The German National Library lists this publication in the National Bibliography; detailed bibliographic data are available on the Internet at http://dnb.dnb.de .

This book is copyright material and must not be copied, reproduced, transferred, distributed, leased, licensed or publicly performed or used in any way except as specifically permitted in writing by the publishers, as allowed under the terms and conditions under which it was purchased or as strictly permitted by applicable copyright law. Any unauthorized distribution or use of this text may be a direct infringement of the author s and publisher s rights and those responsible may be liable in law accordingly.

Imprint:

Copyright © 2009 GRIN Verlag, Open Publishing GmbH
Print and binding: Books on Demand GmbH, Norderstedt Germany
ISBN: 978-3-668-12618-3

This book at GRIN:

http://www.grin.com/en/e-book/313595/a-critical-review-of-stephan-bax-s-article-the-end-of-clt

Mohamed Ben Nasr

A Critical Review of Stephan Bax's Article "The End of CLT"

GRIN Publishing

GRIN - Your knowledge has value

Since its foundation in 1998, GRIN has specialized in publishing academic texts by students, college teachers and other academics as e-book and printed book. The website www.grin.com is an ideal platform for presenting term papers, final papers, scientific essays, dissertations and specialist books.

Visit us on the internet:

http://www.grin.com/

http://www.facebook.com/grincom

http://www.twitter.com/grin_com

A Critical Review of Stephan Bax's Article: The End of CLT: A Context Approach to Language Teaching

The last century has observed remarkable developments in the variety of teaching methods. The reason why such changes happen all the time seems to be the convention that all previously adopted methods did not fulfil all requirements of language learning. In the context of the communicative language approach, in spite of its enormous spread worldwide and its dominance on language teachers today, a number of linguists and teachers suggest that it is time to replace CLT with a more efficient and productive method.

Bax (2003) argues that although CLT has served the language for quite a long time in different aspects, it has however ignored one vital element in language learning, namely the context in which the learning process takes place. Furthermore, he continues to claim that it is prime time to replace CLT as a perfect paradigm with a more suitable and rewarding approach such as a context approach. (Bax, 2003)

This essay has been divided into three main sections. The first section will give a brief description of CLT and its initial purpose followed by a number of contrasting arguments and attitudes. This section is summarised by some comments on Bax's view towards CLT.

The second section sheds lights on the context approach and its properties which is seen by Stephen Bax as a better alternative paradigm to CLT. The validity of this approach is evaluated critically through its characteristics.

The last section suggests some strategies and puts forward certain criteria which may help teachers adopt the most appropriate method according to students' needs and weaknesses.

The core purpose of this essay is therefore to generally agree with Bax's view concerning the crucial importance of learning about the local context in relation to language learning. However, there will be some comments on this approach as to test the possibility of applying it in the future.

Communicative Approach

- The Role of CLT in Learning a Language

The emergence of CLT by the 1980's is said to be the result of the shortcomings observed in the previously adopted approaches. After applying it for quite a long time, some teachers were somehow convinced that all teaching methods such as the Audio-Lingual Method, the Grammar Translation Method and the Direct Method partly failed to cover some of the students' needs in terms of developing their personal skills. In other words, each of the above mentioned approaches has only a main focus which was believed to be the major cornerstone on which other skills could be built. (Bax, 2003, 278)

When CLT emphasizes communication as a major key to language learning, it actually, by doing so, seeks independence for its students to develop their language skills more effectively through interactive courses. Through pair work activities and peer reviews, students would have better opportunities to become more involved in daily conversations as well as working on their weaknesses based on peer reviews and the feedback of the teacher from time to time.

- Contrastive Views About CLT

Swan, M., (1985) discusses the idea that the communicative approach ignores a vital element in language learning; namely the function of L1 in understanding a foreign language. He, however, contradicts this idea saying that teachers inside the classroom feel uncomfortable when they have to be passive in the classroom. He continues to argue that language learning would be more rewarding if classroom activities reflect a real life as far as possible.

Similarly, Harmer J., (2003) assumes that "the problem with communicative language teaching (CLT) is that the term has always meant a multitude of different things to different people". He presumes that proponents of this method share a belief that CLT is communication exercises which are the ultimate solution for language acquisition.

- Bax's Attitude Towards CLT as a Teaching Method

Bax's main argument about CLT is that although CLT has worked quite efficiently to the benefit of language learning, it has not however paid much attention to the context in which the learning process takes place. In other words, context matters were of secondary importance while its priority was to concentrate on developing communication as a tool to improve students' language competence. Furthermore, he suggests that CLT started to have counterproductive results on the profession to the extent that it has to be returned to second place where it belongs. (Bax S., 2003)

In his article, Bax postulates three main statements that emphasise the necessity of changing CLT as "our main paradigm". His first statement is that the communicative approach tries to convince its advocates that the only way of receiving immediate results from language teaching all over the world regardless of the context in which the learning process takes place is through communication. The writer concludes that this message gives the licence for the teacher to manipulate the class in his/her own style in order to create communication. (ibid)

The second statement emphasises a more impressive power of the CLT. It says that all students' learning difficulties and language problems could be sorted out through choosing a suitable method which meets students' needs. Therefore, Bax could notice a counterproductive influence on the teaching profession. The reason, he thinks, is the neglect of the context or the dominance of teaching approach over it. (Bax S., 2003)

The final statement, the writer concludes about CLT, indicates that variation in contexts is not a big issue as long as the teacher has adopted the right methodology. In other words, the CLT today is seen by many teachers as the perfect method which would work efficiently regardless of the context where the language is taught. He summarises the whole three messages commenting that CLT is all about methodology and it is the ultimate solution for all classroom problems. (ibid)

- Critical Evaluation of Bax's Attitude Towards CLT

From the above, it could be understood that CLT may work productively but in very limited kind of social contexts, usually English native speaking countries only. However, saying that does not indicate anyway that such a method should be neglected or less prioritised. As the writer suggests by the end of his article, good teachers can make this approach more rewarding by applying some necessary modifications to suit all cultural differences and meet students' needs and wishes. Furthermore, Bax ultimately calls for a shift in adopting a new teaching approach namely the Context Approach which combines context with language system.

Nevertheless, students' variable abilities to express and observe their needs might be a strong argument for CLT. Inside the classroom, it could be claimed that less gifted students are unlikely to see their weaknesses while they are involved in classroom activities. This is usually the responsibility of teachers to observe the students' weaknesses, or perhaps it is the classmates' through peer reviews and team work and this is exactly what CLT is all about.

Context Approach

- The Definition of a Context According to Bax

Throughout the whole article, Bax discusses the idea of paying more attention to the context and emphasises that Context Approach is the correct paradigm to language teaching. It is yet not clear cut whether this context includes individual potentials of students or it is more about the society in which the learning process takes place. (Bax S., 2003)

- Aspects of Context Variation (How Contexts Vary From Each Other)

According to Bax, the concept of the Context Approach rests on several factors. His list consists of two aspects of contexts. On one occasion, he mentions students' attitudes, needs and wishes. On another occasion, he explains the context as differences in culture, education system, behaviour and probably different methodologies. (Bax S., 2003)

These factors seem to be unlimited and haphazard. If the writer means by contextual factors those related to the study or work environment then he might be right. Students who study a foreign language in a different region find it extremely important to target their needs according to the environment they are expected to work or live in. However, the problem lies in the students themselves. It is realised that observing one's strengths and weaknesses during the class could be a waste of time, particularly for less gifted students who are still in struggle with the language system itself. The natural solution would then move automatically to the tutor.

On the other hand, if the writer wants to describe that set of beliefs, speculations and ambitions then he could be right. In his book, **An International Approach to English Language Teaching**, John Corbett (2003) declares that, "these beliefs relate to the behaviour of the group, and also to the kinds of things it produces to celebrate or assert its identity and values".

To sum up, paying more attention to the context could be extremely important. However, it is the teacher's duty to encourage contextual activities. Students might not all be able to target their strengths and weaknesses as their language competence may not allow them to do so.

Characteristics of Context Approach

There are several advantages which could be gained by applying the context approach. Some of these essential properties can be inferred from Bax's explanation for the difference between CLT and the Context Approach. Firstly, the comparison, as illustrated by Bax S. 2003, suggests that context approach is applicable to almost all learning situations as it takes it as a priority. Secondly, context approach does not conflict with the rest of language methods. Surprisingly, it considers other methods, including CLT, as contributing tools in the learning process. (Bax S., 2003)

- Bax's View of Context Approach

As he contradicts the CLT for its main focus, Bax seems to defend the context approach through the stating its multi-implications in the classroom. He also claims that while CLT's principal consideration is methodology, the context approach goes beyond this to observe students' private lives and personality to fulfil what they require from language learning. (Bax S., 2003)

- Critical Evaluation of Bax's Attitude Towards Context Approach

Properties of the context approach as shown above seem to be promising and more likely to be of international characteristics. It might be predicted that Bax's attitude towards context approach comes from his convention that CLT has had enough impact on teachers and trainees and it is the right time to focus on the language learning rather than methodology. This may also indicate that Bax was influenced by the small number of CLT teachers who described other methods as "backward". However, there is no clear cut evidence to prove that context approach can have the same impact that CLT has had on its advocators. Such an impact is often regarded as a strong proof of its success.

Choosing a Best Teaching Approach

- The Basic Purpose of a Teaching Method

In order to define successful teaching method properly, it would be more appropriate first of all to have a look at what language learners need from language and what the context, they are likely to live in, is like. Good teachers always try to create a balance between these two criteria.

According to John Trim (1985), language learning involves dealing with students with a wide range of roles. Language learners could be communicators, learners, members of various interlocking social groups or as individuals with different cultures, values and beliefs. From this perspective, the best teaching approach can be evaluated through the degree of fulfilling students' needs and speculations, and this perhaps is the turning point in Bax's attitude towards the context approach.

- Adopting the Best Method

In this context, Bax put forward some assumptions to decide on the possibility of implementing the best method in language teaching. He assumes that when the context approach is used and all contexts are completely analysed, all teaching methods including CLT will not be considered as paradigms. He finally suggests an eclectic approach which might be described as the ideal teaching approach for multi-level classes (Bax S., 2003)

To conclude, the Communicative Approach has become such a popular method which may last for a long term. It is sometimes wrongly assumed that this method would work everywhere regardless of the context. The complete ignorance of context by language teachers would properly have its negative consequences. Bax's claim concerning the necessity of replacing the CLT as a standard teaching paradigm with what he calls it the context approach is largely valid. The last section suggests some guidelines when adopting a teaching method with emphasis on the importance of relating context to methodology. Bax's stress on the priority of contexts in language learning seems to be very convincing. Nevertheless, the success rate of the context approach is widely criticised. Perhaps a wiser solution for the problem of language teaching would be finding the balance between its four dimensions namely, the students' needs, the teacher, the context, and the teaching method.

Bibliography

1- Jeremy Harmer, (2003). ELT Journal: Popular Culture, Methods, and Context. Oxford: Oxford University Press. Volume 57/3
2- John Corbett, (2003). ICE: *LANGUAGES FOR INTERCULTURAL COMMUNICATION AND EDUCATION*: *An Instructional Approach to English Language Teaching*. UK: Multilingual Matters Ltd.
3- Penny Ur (ed.), (2002). *Cambridge Handbooks for Language Teachers: Teaching Large Multilevel Classes*. Cambridge: Cambridge University Press.
4- Stephen Bax, (2003). *ELT Journal*: The end of CLT: a context approach to language teaching. Oxford: Oxford University Press. Volume 57/3

YOUR KNOWLEDGE HAS VALUE

- We will publish your bachelor's and master's thesis, essays and papers

- Your own eBook and book - sold worldwide in all relevant shops

- Earn money with each sale

Upload your text at www.GRIN.com
and publish for free